The Rapids

Yogesh Patel received an MBE in the New Year Honours list 2020. Internationally celebrated, he edits and runs *Skylark Publications UK* as well as a non-profit *Word Masala* project to promote literature. Honoured with the *Freedom of the City of London*, he has LP records, films, radio, a children's book, fiction and non-fiction books, and three poetry collections to his credit. A recipient of many awards, Patel was Poet-of-Honor at New York University in April 2019. Among the many venues he has read in, are the House of Lords and the National Poetry Library.

Patel's writing has appeared in many major literary journals, including PN Review, The London Magazine, Asia Literary Review, Under the Radar, Shearsman, IOTA, Envoi, Understanding, Orbis, The Book Review, and Confluence. He has also appeared on BBC TV and Radio, and in newspapers and magazines. Patel's work also features in The National Curriculum anthology, MacMillan, Sahitya Akademi, and numerous other anthologies across the world. He is currently a Poetry Editor at Ars Notoria and writes regular columns for iGlobal and Confluence.

By profession, Patel is a qualified optometrist and an accountant. Author's Websites are: www.patelyogesh.co.uk and www.skylarkpublications.co.uk

Some previous publications

Poetry
Swimming with Whales, in English
Bottled Ganges, in English
The Manikin in Exile, in English

Children's picture book
Magic Glasses, in English

Non-Fiction
Rough Guide Phrase Book for Hindi, A Penguin series
Free Accounting with Free Software, in English

In Gujarati:
Ahin, a collection of poems in Gujarati
Pagalani Lipi, a collection of short stories in Gujarati

LPs
1. *Teri Yaad Aayee*, Hindi
2. *Geet aur Ghazal*, Hindi
3. *Tahukar*, Gujarati
4. *Dōōr-kinārā*, Gujarati

Films/Radio Plays:
The Last Days of Gandhi, In English, Kumbho Films (for NBC)
Companions Forever, BBC Radio 4

Also included internationally in numerous anthologies

The Rapids

Yogesh Patel

The London Magazine Editions
11 Queen's Gate
London
SW7 5EL
United Kingdom

The Rapids

Published by The London Magazine Editions
11 Queen's Gate
London
SW7 5EL
United Kingdom

Copyright ©2021 Yogesh Patel

The right of Yogesh Patel to be identified as the author of this work has been asserted by him in accordance with the Copyright, Design and Patent Act 1988

ISBN 978-1-9196181-7-3

Printed and bound in Great Britain and through various channels internationally for a local distribution.

A CIP record for this book is available from the British Library

Cover painting by Steven Heffer
Design and type setting by TLM Editions

All rights reserved. This book contains material protected under the International and Federal Copyright Laws and Treaties. Any unauthorised reprint or use of this material is prohibited. No part of this book may be reproduced or transmitted in any form or by any means, electronic or mechanical including photocopying recording.

Find out more about The London Magazine at:
Thelondonmagazine.org/tlm-editions

Acknowledgements:

Imtiaz Dharker, Steven O'Brien,
Fiona Sampson, and George Szirtes
for the endorsement and support; I remain in their debt

Steven Heffer
for creating these exquisite paintings on rapids

Rachael Allen
for helping to shape up this oeuvre

Philip Richard Hall
for the final proofs

Debjani Chatterjee, Brian D'arcy, Rishi Dastidar,
and Jason Reading
for championing the new poetic form, the Rapids

Thanks to editors of magazines and anthologies for publishing some of these poems, especially, The London Magazine, Stand, Shearsman, Royal Literary Fund, Writer's Mosaic, India's Sahitya Akademi, Todd Swift's Blogs, Ars Notoria, Dragonfly, INNSAEi, Pratik, Life and Legend, Hope Works, Nirala, and Pippa Rann Books

Poet's special gratitude to

Supported using public funding by
ARTS COUNCIL ENGLAND

for the grant award to develop this opus

**And everything away from literature
a dedication**

to my twins

Malhar and Mrudang
&
their life
Priya and Varsha

&
My dearest granddaughter
Lara
for arriving in 2021 to break the clouds of gloom

Index

The Rapid: Cogito, ergo sum	9
Sweet worms	10
Kafka's Letters	12
Chappals	19
Luminosity	20
Hofstadter's Strange Loop	21
9 out of 10 are men	22
Altitudinal hemianopia	23
The salmon run	24
An eco-warrior	25
Fireflies	26
ゼニー Zen(ī)	27
Tr{oo}ping the Colour	28
Back to normal	29
It'll be Alright on the Night	30
A deflected ritual	31
A milkman's round	33
A theory of social distancing	34
Not an earth-apple, not a love apple	35
The cuffs and bangles	36
Clotho's tangled threads	37
The Book of us	38
Wife Eats Chilli	39
Lost conkers	40
Thali	41
Exquisite Corpse	42
$\Delta S \geq 0$	43
Arrangement	45
The Anger Management	47
Effects	48
The Mono Lake	49
A florid breakup	50
The uncertainty principle	51
All paradises can do with Wendy Cope	52
Not from Mars, not from Venus, they're Made in China	53

It's only a Paper Moon	54
What goes around, comes around	55
Restoration	57
The blank papers of Sadako's 1000 wishes of cranes	59
To write what a tree couldn't	60
The Galatea effect	61
Chicken George	62
Ego death	63
Bone farms	64
Politics of shearers	65
Lions in Trafalgar Square	66
A game of twigs	67
A turn of an hourglass	69
Internet down: Throbbers & Surdarshana Chakra	70
Just as well, 4th Earl of Sandwich didn't meet Anne Boleyn!	71
The Myth of Sisyphus: Camu	72
Wobbling-Belly Laughing Buddha	73
Retirement	74
A quest for art	76
MS	77
The optimist	79
Mautam	80
Kalinga War	81
Notes (1) The Rapid: A New Poetic Form	82
Notes (2) References	86

I say unto you: one must still have chaos in oneself to be able to give birth to a dancing star.

-Nietzsche

The Rapid: *Cogito, ergo sum*

Go for a treasure hunt   in a fragmented poet
Where am I?   *"Love cannot live without trust."*
Psyche heartbroken   *Find me*, I'll be
disconnections: images, legends
I am rules   chaos in a pirouette

Thunder River   a torrent-in-kicks

Sweet worms

I'll take a pen with me
        draw around trees onto sky
illustrate branches
        give them nests:
herons, wrens with machine-gun trills
warblers fluting in allegro and goldfinches with verses
And to mystify where I think I belong
I'll use light-dragged charcoal darkness

I'll sketch the Orphic Egg
to hatch in one of the nests
built by a migratory passerine
The trees branching as sky-veins will also need a flock
       so I'll draw the nomadic birds
            like the ones
                  that sing of sweet worms
                      from back home
To make them aliens   I'll daub them in smudges
      pulled out of the African forest
                like me
           They would have flown oceans
miles   tearing through lightning-whipped clouds
            dodged Khodumodumo like winds
    forgotten their nest   now hunted as Actaeon

Therefore   I'll also draw mega-zoom binoculars
      To show you
           how shivering bodies
                take them from one nest to the other
                  to compose new tunes

Kafka's Letters

Exposition:
Crow: *If the death is so important, why won't you die?*
God: *I have died many an avatar.* सम्भवामि युगे युगे (*sambhavāmi yuge yuge*)
Crow: *There you go: a cheat.*

I
A loss and death can speak in any park.

A cortege of horse chestnut trees
squirrels and magpies watch a dead robin.
A song that once made a happy world is gone.
Is such death pointless?
No one listens to the raven circling above.
Death's meaning is lost in God's avatars.
So, I won't let your thoughts go.
I am not here for a dead song!
I need to cross the avenue and go
to the other side where I still
hear the flock of migrant birds
making sure they must sing.

II
One knows one can't repeat Ruru and Priyamvada's story...

Pandora's Box

The way I walk in the park, in triangles
asked if zigzagging is a ritual,
I say   *the dead robin must have tried*
to pick up straws of tree-broken
sheared light   to build the nest.

A home's not built   on stalks of rays

III
So how does one move on?
Pick up robin's dead body and let the Wandle take it away?

Lethe

Not everyone can be poetic about
Merwin's optimism   wishing to plant
a last tree on doomsday:
the last tree.   We lose someone:
currents take away a body in their

incapacity   to recollect.

IV
But the water can remember by becoming ice!

Icicles

Venus dries off after a dip
in the Wandle.   Stands as
a snow-clad desire.   Neptune in the park
back turned   looks at the walled theatre.
Life wants to rain and thaw.

Recasts   Tsurara-onna.

V
Why must your memories be *psychopomps*?

Reminds Hatfield's Snuff Mill
in the Morden Hall Park
horses once pulled   grumbling millstones
Birds perched   Choked on snuff
Crows too   challenging God

Death needs no reason   just tools

VI
The passing away leaves us with the swan-paddling.
Watermill shows me how repeated scoops fail
as I have, in garnering memories
slipping away from my fingers.
Waterwheels preach,
'What you can't gather, let go.'
- the sages don't always follow their preaching!
They carry on with their labour.
So do I
rummaging around psyche's loft.

VII
How to escape memories' loops?

Under the floorboards!

The loneliness wants to take me
to a park in Surat where grandpa
is not holding my hand anymore
Grandma was gone   I was there
Not every Dora gets Kafka's

Letters   They   wait in the attic...

VIII

A retreat into the garret is not an escape!
A cobweb's silver lines remind you,
the strings of nostalgia form a noose in waiting.
I pull out the letters
with the quaking touch that was a lotus on your face once.
I unfold them the way only love can, careful not to tear,
then pick some random words
to construct renewed meanings
like poker-faced stones turning into God's idols,
waiting to be worshipped.
No word should lose its story in a long unbearable sentence.
I whistle our melody and try to brush it on them.
As our tune refuses to become mine, as destined,
I let it go to the bouncing ball
to allow it to jump a rhythm on revived syntax
packed with the ghosts from your letters.
Let a blackbird join. A chaffinch can sing too.
There is a lot of deathly silence to fill
with their Garuda Purana chants for you.
A melody is better at celebrating love
than the rasping chorus of heartaches!

IX
I should walk downstream, as that would be life.
Instead, I saunter upstream,
watching past left as the ruins of a long brick wall
which plays tricks to remind us
what we had also has a unique timeline.
The remains allow us to linger on a bit more
or trap us in their era.
But the bricks will be dust one day.
What will happen to the pain that would still haunt?
Will it be a disease like the Wandle's bygone current
a sewer in the mid-19th century,
a conduit for typhoid and cholera?
An aeon may cure things, we are told.
The stalker, the past, must be arrested.
The death must be left as punctuation in the continuum.
The water knows this, runs detached,
has no need for Kafka's letters, *an arrangement*,
to let go the Doll!

X

All hearts should be Morden Hall Park
where Dora could come every day: cry;
tell Kafka, *'I've lost my doll,'* [1]
and wait for him
to shield her from a loss or death
to bring her a letter from her Doll
believed to have gone far away.

But the story cannot end without
Kafka bringing the last letter
that would not tell her–dolls die too
not like Avatars, but like robins, Grandma, and you.
A child in us would always want a smiling end!
So, one day, we would want the Doll to marry a young man.
We won't go into happily-ever-after
for no one knows if the young man was turned into a frog
waiting for his kiss...

XI
If you ever get a chance, listen to the crow zigzagging above

when something we love is lost
we can find something else, words
which will bring it back to us
and we will never lose it again.[1]

and that loss can't hide behind Avatars
we all need   Kafka's letters

Denouement:

God: (Jeremiah 23:23)
*I am God who is
everywhere and not
in one place only.*
अहम् ब्रह्मास्मि (Ahaṁ Brahmāsmi)
> *Therefore, I haven't lost anything*

>> *So what is   this hurt?*

*
> To that
>> crow wants to laugh, but can't.

---

[1]*From Kafka's Doll in Zigzag by Anthony Rudolf. In this story, Kafka finds a girl, Dora, in a park, crying, as she has lost her doll. Kafka devises daily letters, with the final letter to give closure to the girl's loss.*

Chappals

It wasn't the first time they had come with me.
We arrived at the door
turned the keys
stepped inside, rubbed footwear on the mat.
As usual, to haunt me
Chappals parked themselves in
the silence of a corridor.
Dropping on the sofa, I ignored them as before.

As a Hindu, I can't visit a grave
take flowers,
the ache desperate to perform.
Instead, a burning incense
throws a pashmina smoke-scarf
winding in anger to noose memories.
The knickknacks on the dressing table
perhaps knew you better.
They meditate as Buddhist monks
with tantric words hanging expectantly.

Even mornings remember you better than I can!
So, every day, the breakfast cutlery tinkles
to get chappals ready for a walk with me.
But I walk out the door
leave them on the mat as always;
an unforgivable habit too late to correct now.
Yet timidly as a shadow - as always - they follow me.

Luminosity

dribbles from trees,
the Sun trying to slurp up the dew,
the precipitation of last night's cold longing.
The brilliance flows
to cure the left-over love's anguish.
On the branches, I see an affectionate ghost
in the shape of a smashed vase
which cannot hold the weight of any bloom.
Waves light disturbed by a diving swallow.
Solid blades of grass stiff with frost
remind me of our past, exchanged anger
still coming back to terrorise with small yearning grazes.
I can break my bygone annoyance
by walking on a rug of iced memories on the pathways.
They crackle, make me slip.
The watery vermiculation of hope freed
redraws the shaky lines of my path,
the palm ahead with the predicted grief ambushed.

This is the visual music.
It echoes from the trees
to thaw mornings to last the day.

What do I care?
I only need one good day!
I am elated to walk with these bright rivulets
holding your ghostly snowy hand through planes
icicling through leaves holding mine!

Let me enjoy the luminosity
to prove nothing!

Hofstadter's Strange Loop

Rapids you're in   are only   calm
waters up and down streams
All roads   go stray
unless you know   the destination
A scarecrow keeps   the birds

out   instead   can watch the stars

(Dedicated to www.stretch-charity.org **and Nirala Publication's** *SOS Surviving Suicide*)

9 out of 10 are men

Exile Night is to light a candle
squat in a corner, eat cold food, think of mosquitoes
and geckos crawling on the ceiling to fall in my soup
and wonder why them nights are here again and love is
somewhere there.

The night is cast in the tarmac-blood
not Anish-Kapoor red.
What I stare is not a sculpture
twisted or raised as an ugly and bloody metaphor.

What we would say always needed a mosquito net.

White flags on the roadmap leading to nowhere.
Where one starts from is not a point of context anymore
you: home   me: boxed   two references

The next day, a snarling municipal refuse truck will collect
and squash up yesterday held together
like a wobbly cardboard box;
the council believes it can always clear the rubbish.
They haven't visited hearts.
I don't know anymore who defines what waste is.

I am supposed to leave the box after every Exile Night.
I leave the coughing loneliness behind
in search of a fresh cardboard assembly.

All because you, in my house, have made sure
I don't deserve a home, only another cardboard box to fold.

Altitudinal hemianopia

the hesitant snow from the Himalayas
runs down as the Ganges
the Yeti swims down laughing
go check where Shiva
danced his climate-tandava

ignore   my   footprints

The salmon run

the untied threads of
magnetoreception
severed natal river smell
salmon can't return to
the womb to hopscotch and breed

a need to find   a new home

An eco-warrior

Shiva's Rudra Tandava overflows.
Its lava streams down a slope

looks into my eyes
scaling heights to clouds!

Don't, it would sadly insist
just don't . . .

Go upstream
you will find rocks.

And you will be alone.
Go downstream;

you will find rivers
cities and finally the ocean

greater than Mount Kailash.
And you won't know where to begin.

The clouds you seek
will be there too

but they won't become an avalanche—
melting glaciers on my jata (जटा)

to flood the world
left only with paper boats to paddle.

Tell me, stranger, however,
why are you after clouds?

Fireflies
Delhi, May 2021

Each plight of sparks		enlightens a crackled sky
Ashes drifting in gasps
The oxygen   never arrived
like promises			and hopes

But there's plenty for Hades
in the hellhole, a car park
though concocted with stench
charred flesh burning		dashed hopes

A doctor comes out for a smoke
but runs back inside
filled with the dead lurking
in his lungs		as ashes

Alfresco		the wood-fireflies
pop in the cloud of fetid smoke
indoors			the unattended dead
wait under the sign		*No Smoking*

ゼニー Zen(ī)

water runs free,   not
to memorise experienced   *dvaita*
not to go forward to learn
joyous carp   leaping over
Dragon's Gate   to be a dragon

anglers waiting   to hook the river

Tr{~~oo~~}ping the Colour

I am always getting   undone
like my shoelaces
tr{ip}ping   pranāma   to catch bruises
looking up   to find   a daisy smiling:
'You should've been careful.'

Hate those who   speak the obvious

Back to normal

It is not a fruit.
But it has fallen off the tree with a stone.
Just because it has fallen off the tree
it is categorised as a fruit.
For days, no one bothered.
The rumour is moths ate all leaves.
The trees mutated as the viruses do!
These latest nuts have plagued the grounds I walk on.
Squirrels cannot classify the pits for their need.
Despairing, they all huddle up on roads quiet
in the pandemic.
The conference like all others ends in disagreements.
They all agreed to ignore the rare pits
as nature's bizarre idea!
Though they must be all happy
having had the chance to read their papers without Zoom.
They returned to their brushwood
in search of routine conkers like all academics
waiting to see what happens to the odd harvest.
With squirrels deserting the roads,
I feel safe now from rabies.
Though, not from the roads overrun with the excess crop.
All politics played, the council removed them.
The arborists found the treatment, sprayed the trees, and killed the lab moths.
In the world of conkers, it is now easy for me
to come and see you.
But as before,
I will only text you.

It'll be Alright on the Night

A bargain	An offer from COVID
2021	half lockdown
Buy 2 Get 1	Half Price
Clotted Brexit	Devon cream?
502	A bad gateway
Once the sale ends	Reboot!

A deflected ritual

Everyday
on the same branch
the two Xeroxed egrets
perched on the tree
sitting at a distance
                                        in silence.

They sit like lovers post-quarrel.
They watch clouds.
They wrestle with their propinquity.
Wonder; how far is *far enough*?

I am on a bench
next to the rushing Wandle
watching moments studded
on that gliding   foggy milky way
readying itself to get dispersed
in the enormous wheels of a heritage watermill
captive in its monotonous time loop
where history still echoes
but gets on with the inevitable.

A seat on the tree is empty.
The lovers must have buried the hatchet.
To shed loneliness
the tree has foliaged:
one gets on with life.

The same branch:
Egrets have not returned.

Then one autumn
leaves fall
a curtain goes up
the carbon-copy egrets return.

A pigeon ousted as a squatter knows
Sisyphus needs to let the boulder go:
walk down the other side of a mountain.
It splashes my bench with its droppings:
Time to change the seat.

A milkman's round

history doesn't repeat bottles
at four in the morning as it used to
now I stumble over empties we collected
at the doors we erected as monuments
the change is a clock without keys

to wind back for   fresh orders

A theory of social distancing

We invent our myth and pure theories and we try them out: we try to see how far they take us.

- Karl Popper

Don't look me up in any thesis.
To understand, you won't need to read me over and again.
I am in the workings of everything
one of the sneaky forces
running in unison
and prompting our universe
to deliver algorithms correctly.

So, if you can handle that premise
we can find
what the theory of special relativity didn't solve:
a fresh mathematical statement
that will help us understand
why we are still holding arms
and wandering aimlessly
in the field of otherness.
Our social distancing
can have a fresh equation
but of all ideas, I prefer
to sit with you and laugh
at a dinner table and observe your empty chair.
Do you have a theory about
loneliness trapped in a bottle of Shiraz
I can pour for us to enjoy
while humanity squanders its time
trying to understand the Vedic philosophy of *māyā* (माया)?

Not an *earth-apple*, not a *love apple*

I won't pick it on command
I will wait for the apple to drop
There aren't any schemes   plots
for me to discover Gravity
The Garden of Eden   Snake's gone

to Samudra   Manthan

The cuffs and bangles

tearing a paper was easy
the right piece   got a house
the left bit   took a sea
I hadn't drawn   you
fish and I   were with the sea

with gulls on the right   fish escaped

Clotho's tangled threads

She was Jenga   and yet too many
bricks were pulled out   dominoes falling
she lay scattered   for those with rods
as a t#rn sari   once dipped in a rainbow
Adikia bloody   on the ground

Trying to split   Dike's staff

(Dedicated to all rape victims)

The Book of us

it was an old book
wisdom of us cast away
Buddha   with Bodhi Vriksha
Arjun   & Krishna's Gita
but the dry leaves   treeless

thrived sandwiched as ossified words

Wife eats chilli

    hats off to chilli it could do what i can't
      the lashing sun   on the tongue

  what am I to do?   i am but just a man
can't sing, in a gondola, 'just one cornetto.'
    a salute to   the silencing chilli

  i can be ice cream   but am just a biscuit

Lost conkers

Each day rakes at something in me.
The pushed-away breakfast walks out in silence
leaving me as in crumbs on the table!
One day, when this is not the case
I hope you'll come and sit with me
on a bench that lets me count
the days merge seamlessly like mist:
as humans must in love.
Time-drenched water drags murmurs.
I have learnt from it how to mumble!
Like me, it has made journeys only to forget.
I don't see redundant leaves on the bank; I see words.
They cover the mud, which must hide.

There is nothing here that is
the Ganges, the Thames or the Nile;
their ascension is an ocean
to lose themselves through expatriation
as love should.
I'll shuffle, wink and smile.
Invite you into my ultimate exile
on the embankment of a flow that claims one name
but ends up with another!
Not love but a submission.
We will survey the past running around
like squirrels mapping and hiding conkers
and with a clap disappearing from the view
Whitman's gulls surveying and laughing:
Hide the conker, find the conker; it's a game lost:
me and me, you and me, and you and you.

Thali

We came together in a pledge
with an allusion of gravity
you winning most coins
in a wedding-game *thali*.

Eyes locked, sentences with *bindi*,
we talked around *thali*.
The aroma absorbed our pasts
in *daal*, *roti* and *bhaji*.

Thali now spins:
centrifugal forces
at work, words are
coins flying like bullets!

Exquisite Corpse

It was a fine campfire of me
my image was built in a *Consequences* preset
like Jumanji I'm where I'm not
E.T. can't go home from the *Exquisite Corpse*
All games end at some point to reboot

Just wait for Prometheus   to steal the fire

$\Delta S \geq 0$

We are face to face: high and low entropies.

The flowers you bring are burdened with scent.
You smile with a salesperson's rattling grin.
You have locked yourself into time that is high entropy,
tossed the keys in the Vaitarani,
so you cannot come back. But here you are now!
You smile and assure me, it is the same smile
you smiled years ago. Time doesn't play that way.
I wish I can stop it as anglers can.
But time is not a rod –
it is an arrow: that's an old smile you are wearing
and I am the new boring I am carrying!

Thermodynamics of love means
you are not = but must unleash to >.
Ω is not the same as ॐ.
Love can be Ω and it can be also ॐ.
So you're welcome to Quantum Mechanics.
I want you to thrive simultaneously, but of course,
you don't understand it!
You have come to talk about an instant
as that picture on a wall
the moments hanging stuck in zero
in the unyielding equation.
You offer the point at which nothing else exists
for me, you and us.
In fact, you have come to cash in on the present!
Prof. Carlo Rovelli says *now means nothing*!
So, should I entertain you as the present?
You try to make me believe in his *spacetime cones*.
You deviously keep your message simple: *Come back to me.*

The chequebook doesn't fit the quantum theory:
it needs a specific date.
It can't be *I love you*
When it is *you owe me*!
So, I say, of course, I will come back to you,
but I'll leave the cheque book here.

The bees are tucking into yesterday's cold pizza
we left untouched.
Now, here I am with the agitated entropy of sadness
making time a future's fool, confused,
and resorted to decay with our leftover pizza!

Arrangement

You came to see me.
We convened, stitching the void.
Your eyes covered.
I could not tell if you were protecting
a stranger or me!

We struggled to place ourselves in a mural:
a brook coiling the valleys
with hills locked in a coitus
as if they were feeling elated
and didn't know lust from love!
For you, it was important to talk.
You wanted everything like your idea of a painting:
fixed colours, well-composed.

You always apprehended us in a gallery.
The painting had to be in shades of grey:
The black firmer, the grey shifting like a cloud.
One watching, one an exhibit.
You would say colours are noise
like unruly children.
Shapes we created were smoky fires
glowing embers as habaneras.
The lines smudged like ghosts
trying to create an impression
not an assertion: a good hiding place, I suppose.
You would dismiss any Picasso, saying,
anything that is a cube is a suspicious chest.

The house on the wall even now
stands with expectations
in sad, light-starved colours.

Inside, burns some warm firewood
with maybe a cat and a dog in a nap.

But it was a house behind drawn curtains
that forgets colours, where trees grow
into wildwood.

That is when I learnt
how words string us along:
always pugnacious!
They coil our gorges
betraying any meaning
because they know
how to escape a picture
The way they want!

I get up, draw a taxi as a signature
in the driveway of a house:
the door of a taxi left open civilly.
Calmly, I walk out.

The anger management

The darkness is a congenital liar
Let the words ignite a yagna-fire
The moons hide with "fake" light
A single diya can brighten the night
Let the words find their mother tongue

To engulf lava   Kali's tongue

Effects

With a photo-app trick you
crossed the *threshold,* changed the house.
Words *rippled* it with effects.

A paper moon added *soft edges.*
Love was still shearing through
the *shutters* effect; there was no window.

The *zoom blur* allows a distance.
You insist it is *sunshine* and *glow:*
my view is through *glass tiles!*

I wildly held the *mosaic* together.
Now just want the *pencil effect*
so I can colour my {lost} home...

The Mono Lake

two strangers sitting in the same room
immersed in own bubble-submarines
in a saline soda lake of deep silence
even Mark Twain wouldn't have enjoyed
watching these Mono Lake flies
avoiding a look at each other

the silence feels as old as the briny lake
now made shallow with a seasonal change
so these strangers can walk alone underwater
in their spacesuit-isolation
the room-lake also offers words-brine-shrimps
sustains its ecosystem

we are them, and they are us
we are also a part of the food chain
birds   deceptively sweet   as a family watching us
are like a tribe of Kutzadika'a
you have assembled
not realising they all gorge on vulnerable flies

now you laugh that
this fly will leave the basin
and the bastard law has bequeathed
the whole salt lake to you

to your head-banging annoyance
i look happy to let go of the alkali lake
for what i know and you don't
love is not always the salt of life

A florid breakup

As you leave, they try to paint you as a rotter.
Outside, a carpet of autumn leaves rolled out for you
reminds you of shades of lies you'll walk on
while *bumblebee orchids,*
naked man orchids,
snapdragon seed pods, snigger
at a looser;
lies becoming truth under the influence.
Facts have no loyalties;
they depend on versions of
the common stinkhorn and
how many trellises they
grab at a party…

Good luck, you say.
You smile.
Free at last in the fragrance
of *night-blooming jasmine*
in friendly black space
I try to define as freedom.

All flowers are free to smile in a season.
All florid breakups mark a season's end.
The *jasmine* reminds you,
there can be a thriving alternative in every night
while it is best to leave the *jakkalskos* alone
to thrive underground, leafless,
be unknown to the daylight or a fresh breeze.

The uncertainty principle

the bell rings loud enough
        not for your ears
camera sends video
        only for your eyes
the bouquet's fragrance eludes

you're there   and not there

Curtains drop

Ranglo enters Bhavai's apron and recites a poem
(Bhavai is a traditional folk-theatre culture of Gujarat. In most Bhavai, Ranglo is a character who performs in stage's apron to break the monotony during the breaks with the comedy. He enters after an act and leaves the forestage for the next instalment of the play.)

All paradises can do with Wendy Cope

Life is *bhavai*   but in the breaks
you need Ranglo   to make you laugh
forestage of life also matters
All theatres   project fictions
All mythologies   make gods human

if deities can't laugh heavens are hell

Not from Mars, not from Venus, they're *Made in China*

        cataracts can give you   rainbows
            so could glaucoma
      vision needs mind   not eyes
      you can stand there   offer visions
          but you watch my watch

      counting thousands   *it's fake, Chinese*

It's only a Paper Moon

I lost my password.
Can't log in to me.

She knows it.
Time to ask has passed.
There is no button to reset it.

A florist can't offer the right flowers.
Jewellers can't please with any old ring.

Anthony Rudolf tells me
there is a case here for selective memory loss!

Then I met a hacker.
A few dates and several glasses of wine,
no password needed,
she tries to hack into my account.

I have now installed an antivirus
a firewall, and an anti-malware.
But where do I keep a password to my passwords?
Another password-protected file to find it?

I am now waiting for a date
who wouldn't need my laptop password
but is happy to share 1981 Chateau Verdignan.

Ranglo leaves the forestage
Curtains go up

What goes around, comes around

It was a pensive *Bosongo* Kisii
still the fifties' Empire a predator.
Boyto would whistle *Malaika* for hours
in the yard making chickens happy
listening, getting fat for the slaughter.

Inside the walls, I wouldn't know he
was the pure descendent of humans
that came from The Great Rift Valley.
Boyto would play with me, tell me stories,
he had five *wives* and no land to claim!

He was happy, but would hold *mapanga*
against Mau Mau assailants
'jifiche, kijana, jifiche.'
One of us, he should have been on the same floor
in the Indian family in Kisii;
Boyto was kept non-Indian!
Shame has many names, not this one.

'Njoo Mvulana, njoo mvulana mzuri'
– Come, boy, come, a good boy –
There! We would chase chickens:
no hatred, just pure fun. A chase.
Freedom couldn't fly high;
the chicken's faced walls.

At supper, we would lick bones
of the chickens that couldn't jump walls.
Failed freedoms became masala chicken!
Hidden in their wishbones
I didn't break with Boyto
are trapped hisses of wishes.
A child never forgets a friend.
Boyto knew a little witchcraft.

He hid well in my wishes.

He still wanders with me
in the woods of druids;
inside my skin, humming,
'Malaika, nakupenda Malaika'
still heartbroken with no dowry to offer.
He smiles at me, knows
whatever I offer druids, it will be less!

'Kinachoenda, huja, mvulana!' whispers Boyto.
And I agree, *'Nakupenda, Boyto!'*

Swahili glossary:
KISII town was born when the British government set up an administrative post at the District Commissioner's office. The locals called it *Bosongo*.
Bosongo - white man's land *(Abasongo-the white people)*
mapanga- Machete
jifiche,kijana, jifiche hide boy, hide
'Njoo Mvulana, njoo mvulana mzuri' - Come, boy, come, a pretty boy
Malaika A famous African song; girl's name
nakupenda I love you
Kinachoenda, huja, mvulana! What goes around, boy, comes around

(Thanks to writer Abu Amirah of Hekaya Arts Initiative for the help with Swahili. Also to Olatoun of Borders Book Review and Margaret Busby OBE)

Restoration

The empire left me in
a basket in the Nile.

Moses, the foundling, adopted
by Pharaoh's daughter
runs away to be Moses again.
Krishna also kept quiet
in a basket through
the split Yamuna
to grow up with other parents.
The restoration
is a migration,
a boomerang or a dogged
migrant boat in a storm.

Someone like me thanks the fate
for the heartless journey,
a reinstatement,
a wrested return home.
To pass history's baggage
in the never-ending rapids,
while I struggle to balance,
the empire pins a medal on me.
Humbled, a basket still dreams an escape!

There are splits and bends
in the Nile, so it *will be* a sea.
From the seas to the clouds
to the Ganges, to the seas
to the clouds, migration
flows to the Tamesis, Temese, *Tamasa* or Thames
the time marked by a changing name
- Canute's disobedient river -
that refuses its history!

There is no name for such a transfer.
The skep pines for the hands of love.

How do you explain
to the migrant, Wilma the whale,
that the banks of the Thames are also
Harmondsworth prison;
that they lock away disowned
citizens with the wrong colour?
Hope is a game I play;
watch the dust particles
floating in the pencil of light
with which I'd wish
to draw a window, so I can see my home.

There is always hope for
the prisoner transfer: it comes!
I'm a project restoration.
Though I'm glad they've just
found my lost, dusty files.
When I'm let loose
to enter this new home
and the basket beaches as a whale
I seek your help. Please,
if they ask my name,
what should be my answer:

I am Moses

or

I am Krishna?

The blank papers of Sadako's 1000 wishes of cranes

Lilacs' beauty fills the heart
with my mother tongue
The fragrance drifts as
 the se{con}ded language
But the callous plant   wants

wasps   to spread   the potpourri

To write what a tree couldn't

When I witnessed the log adrift
mid-ocean with no schema
shaken by currents, torn between two lands,
on the deck of the SS Karanja,
I learnt my first lesson as a child:
even the trees don't know
where they will end up one day.

They say there is an adventure
in the unknown
but the child always wants to know.

Clutching my British passport
in the Harmondsworth cell
sitting on a squeaking bed
watching a pencil of light
with *pranām* to my feet
I knew there was a hole
in the walls, they had erected.

It was up to me to hold that pencil,
a feather without a bird, write a song
that the tree adrift in the sea couldn't.

The Galatea effect

How wonderful to be
an intruder in these
woods, a shying rivulet pulling away
its reticent wave-sari
to be nobody
amidst dunnocks and blackbirds
engaged in a symphony.
Incongruous,
I am glad to be
accepted by the horse chestnuts, limes and planes,
and the embracing vine climbing, light-headed
and rustling, and reminding me
I am just a migrant
in this part of the world.
Therefore, before the fog erases me,
let me sway with the trees
with earphones crooning Raj Kapoor's
'मेरा जूता है जापानी (Mera Jutta hai Japani)'*
and dance the blast as an oddball;
no one wanting me to be a tree
in this part of the world

---

*(A classic song from Raj Kapoor's 1955 film Shree 420 is about one's ultimate identity.
मेरा जूता है जापानी/ये पतलून इंगलिश्तानी/सर पे लाल टोपी रूसी/फिर भी दिल है हिन्दुस्तानी
My shoes are from Japan, pants from England, my head boasts ushanka, yet at heart, I remain a Hindustani.)

Chicken George

a river splits for my
life's   warring viewpoints
the left stream   chokes in weeds
the right one   is joie de vivre
I keep walking on

dead leaves sun-drowned

Ego death

many a dish I've created
have no names   moments
in dead men's society
one's always an incomplete
Joseph K.   still under

The Bell Jar   ID

Politics of shearers

Spaghetti   grows on trees
BBC broadcasts   a hoax
Fake news   8 million
will buy   like a lottery
      सत्यमेव जयते
    (*Satyameva Jayate*)

A wolf in   sheep's skin?

Bone farms

They planted the bones in this desert
and hoped for the trees.

The rain never tapped words here
dancing on war-bitten roads,
the words that children won't hear.
Yes, tears may rain
but the trees won't grow with them.
One must not give in to the history.
It has no heart, just rubble.
The sky is no longer at peace,
circling Mig-29s are the new falcons.
Their cloud-tails scratch a silver-line.
Damask Roses have fallen to dust
in the only monsoon where bullets rain.
The hands that can plough are all bones
in barbarians' metal-mushroom farms.

Circling Mig-29s are the new falcons.
Their cloud-tails drag a fake silver-line.
They could have simply risen from a hookah
puffed by an old man as a wish
that the clouds he saw once would rain one day,
where prophets planted the bones in this desert
and promised trees.

Lions in Trafalgar Square

I sit and gaze at fountains and pigeons
watching mobile users driving
unable to prosecute   bored
I'm also here   illegally
Lions of Sanchi Capital   lost

Truth locked away   in a museum

A game of twigs

What am I doing on this bridge
dropping twigs to play Pooh-sticks
    disturbing the fabric of spacetime?

Why does it matter if the truth is
      a fragment of
           a bough; dry or green
   yours or mine?
      Dropped as a twig it races to win
   an out-of-control spin.

The truth can defeat you.
      Be a child on a bridge.   Play to win.
        Try over and again.
To master the truth   drop two sticks.
      Choose the one that wins.

I have seen in your stealthy eyes
   an avowal as the seeds of Mahabharata.
      Like you   it is the Ganga
    emerging to bear Bhishma
   to die for the warped truth
as a sage in the name of an oath
     on a bed of arrows in Kurukshetra.

Here we are
playing the Truth.
Don't convince me
with Yudhisthira's hypocrisy
      अश्वत्थामा हतः इति नरो वा कुंजरो वा
     (*Aswatthama Hatah iti Naro va Kunjaro va!*)

Be a friend.
Drop sticks with me
to disturb my rippled image:
no more an image
that twigs can race through.

A turn of an hourglass

how does one go back to normal
when there's no one to return to?
The garden shade has spiders   has hidden beer
    war's over   but the war's come home
when you're lost and when you're pissed

a world is a sniper   you're now a jihadist

(Dedicated to soldiers coming home with PTSD)

Internet down: Throbbers & Surdarshana Chakra

Narad had been missing for days
Vishnu has no clues what the world is up to
No fake news, no Twitter, no BBC
Poor Shesh has no break from His burden
For once Laxmi should drag The Lord to a kitchen

Teach Him Madhur Jaffrey's masala chai

Just as well, 4th Earl of Sandwich didn't meet Anne Boleyn!

"Seldom has any man
held so many offices and
accomplished so little."
I've gambled time   Sandwich watching
Love in a rabbit hole in Iraq

Emerging playing lies   for the Snickers

The Myth of Sisyphus: Camu

old Ezra Pound storms
in ears   bolting me to a floor
should I listen to a poem
or should I justify the noise
as meaning   in life

Sestina: Altaforte

Wobbling-Belly Laughing Buddha

truth is a diamond with laughing facets
the light it reflects hides colours
sun's seven galloping horses
are the runaway rainbow of a fool
the Lion Capital of Ashoka roars

with always at its feet   the massacre of Kalinga

Curtains drop
Ranglo enters Bhavai's forestage and recites a poem

Retirement

In retirement, there needs no connection
between the *ticktock* of a watch
and the kingfisher's-*clickety-clackety* tracks
you chase in the tunnel's belly
using your Freedom Pass
trying to look into leave-me-alone eyes.

Not that there should be anything to see
in a magazine discarded
with glossy beach sand trapped
in the touched-up hourglasses designed
to remind you what is slipping away
while the sea overlooks bearing the burden of
sapphire emptiness
filled with cloud-nines
wanting to snatch-sip your mojito
to make absolutely sure you are left feeling empty!

There is a reason for you to let that sea go free.
Physics will assure you
time has no arthritis on top of a mountain; it moves faster.
A demand from retirement is to have knee pain
and walk along a moment-sluggish beach.

In retirement, ditch the valleys and mountains
hold a bottle of whiskey in your hands
wear your most awful shirt; a kind of
dawning of colour-jazz
flash your hairy flamingo legs from

some torn printed Bermuda shorts
and let the clickety-clackety train
get out of your lonely tunnels
because you know – like you –
TfL also can't cope with rain or snow.

Part-exchange your walking stick for tyres
And know this: time is a gullible customer.

A quest for art

A curator can tell you how and where
you must hang yourself on a wall
as a contentious exhibit.
Don't ask critics. They are cigars.
Or a pompous wine hammocking in a glass.

A librarian can tell you
if you have a place in a selection
on display at a famous library.
Don't ask poets. They are hangovers.
Or emblems in their trophies...

Art can stand giving the finger
the blaring ArcelorMittal Orbit!
Your wife is your best critic. She'll tell you,
having a voice is a sure way to perish.
Embrace: art unfolds in silence!

Ranglo leaves the forestage
Curtains go up

MS
(Dedicated to Jo and Jeremy Piper)

You're showing me a wrecked world.
It's chaos harnessed as a painting;
a kaleidoscope of the rainbow-shards
we had to toss into random autumn leaves
covering the space we have been left with.
I have now framed the canvas to avoid further ripping.
I stroke your hands gently:
This is you who once wandered off for some meaning.
You muse: *Can you see the rearranged fragments as love?*

You filled the chopped emptiness of the sky
and mosaic of the sea
with shaky brushstrokes of fire.
The contrasts can sometimes present something in common.
I walk sideways; I study from an angle;
I examine the rapports of what we have crystallised.
Bloody things are disconnected
You reassure me:
These are opposite worlds of sky and sea, and in abundance,
fallen and shattered in sparklers
You've to learn to see their yogic balance of assimilation.

Then you gently pull back your hand
Nothing is shattered, and yet everything is.
Not everything dropped shatters. What we see broken,
doesn't have to be the art of Kintsugi of old hierarchy.
The meaning can come from the rearrangement of the art of living.

The light was touching the frame.
I forgot to put the Sun in this clutter.
Hold my shaky hands with a brush.
Help me put a dab of yellow where it creates a void.

But the pain has its lexicon.
Your hand's sea waves couldn't reach the shores
to drop a shell.
Like humans, the sun can't wait. It moves on.

Some things are best left alone, contained in their meaning.
We agree.
The time had come for a painting to hang and be itself
without a need of any blithering, interfering suns.

The optimist

I will not have just LED star dot lights in the sky.
Starlings will have to bring some too –
blackbirds ferrying light in their feathers!

To experience the shiver, the thrill
to feel the adrenaline from life on the run
I would add falcons to this sky.

I'm not worried about the hawks.
They can have rodents on the land
getting fatter and bigger like human rats!

Hawks don't sing.   They're not invited!
I will not have just the stars in the sky
starlings *will have to* come and *sing*.

Mautam

Life needs to self-destruct to revive
drown in a rat-flood's recurrence
Hope devours dreams that dream dreams

All pompous hollow bamboos will fall
the rat-flood will deny the regimes their wind
with no warbling *bansuri* left for songs

then will arrive the believers without books
to collect plant seeds on blank pages
to raise a forest for the aspirate flutes

the fate will create the *bansuri* for Krishna
or summon the *Pied Piper* of Hamelin
the rats will follow the rats, will follow

Mautam to follow Mautum to deforest
the order and reforest the chaos for
hope to play the new *bansurian*

(Mautam is a phenomenon that recurs every 40-50 years in northern Indian states of Tripura, Mizoram and Manipur. The abundance of Bamboo seeds falling during Mautam creates a plague of rats called a rat flood. They destroy the forest and cause a famine. That reshapes politics and life in the region.)

Kalinga War

*it's a bullet
crow's eye
god in the line of fire*

*in each man's pocket
the crow has slipped
a warring gun*

*the crow is watching
god's funeral
at a Dakhma*

*crow knows
each man will collect
god's remains*

*start a shrine
an avant-garde religion
a weapon*

*but the hopes are hopes
and god made the man
in His image
to dream with His eyes
hence, be unknown to crow
at Kalinga the man is now
aiming at the crow*

Notes (1)
The Rapid: A New Poetic Form

The Rapid is a new form developed by Yogesh Patel. The prime test for a good Rapid is *jostles, disorientation and excitement of a Thunder River Rapids Ride*! This is a jazz of poetry. It is a hallucination that weirdly makes sense! These are the poems on the run, ideas falling on each other occasionally, shaken and stirred. Therefore, just the rules of this form do not make the Rapids! However, to drill the commotion, the form has rules.

The core rules:
- As the poem is a 5-1 sestet of short lines
- The maximum line length is accentual tetrameter. If shorter, try to maintain a pattern.
- As no exception to the rule, the sixth line must be in tetrameter, accentual or otherwise, separate and must be split equally in the middle as 2-2
- The two-stress end phrase helps on its own in extending the allegory being handled
- The title increments poem's meaning. It is not a repeat of the theme.
- Along with disrupted connectivity, the suggestiveness through metaphorical, folklore or mythical stories and characters is an important aspect of this form

Here is what some poets who have enjoyed writing it have to say:

Liberate to the point of anarchy

All poems have structure—even blank verse and free verse. A good poem is one in which structure and content are seamlessly married and the poet simultaneously enjoys a sense of freedom in creating the poem. A poem fails when the reader notices these requirements are not realised. I have always found of interest such traditional forms as the ghazal, the villanelle, and the sonnet; so, I was naturally drawn to the Rapid, a new arrival in the world of poetry (Yogesh Patel invented it in 2020). It can rival any traditional form in its stringent requirements of length, metre and format. But what I find so remarkable about this form is that it can also be liberating to the point of anarchy! The freedom of expression that it offers can mislead one into thinking that the Rapid is a quick and easy option; but I would caution all poets bold enough to essay this form. The Rapid too is much more than the sum of its structure and layout. Its subject matter and revelation are important. Its teasing, its insight and its surprise element, the enjoyment in the ghazal couplet-like individuality and connectivity of each Rapid line - all these are part and parcel of this challenging new form of poetry.

-Dr Debjani Chatterjee MBE FRSL

How to surf a poetic rapid

A new form to grab this intense, mixed up world, fast; here's how to write a rapid:

Step 1: Listen to your heartbeat, four times. De-dum. De-dum. De-dum. De-dum. That's the gallop to hit.

Step 2: Grab something, everything and anything that might be around you. Distil it into four lines.

Step 3: Concentrate now. Pour what you've surfed into something smaller – that's line 5.

Step 4: Find your focus, the revelation, the drop. That's line number 6.

Step 5. Take that line, give it some air. Tab a gap between your first two beats and your last.

Step 6: Leap back up. Set a riddle or a jump beyond for your title. Paddle hard. Catch the wave.

-Rishi Dastidar

Distract, divert, connect, and clarify!

It is not every day that a new and refreshing poetic form emerges. So, welcome to the new world of the Rapid, with thanks to Yogesh Patel for the new world discovery! All you need for the voyage is the imagination and discipline to reveal an insight into your world within 'six' lines of formatted iambic tetrameter; lines that:

1. Individually distract and divert, but
2. collectively connect and clarify with the title plus final, heavily formatted, line serving to:
   > Drop the anchor,   Seal the voyage.
3. Finally, and hopefully, reveal something revealing of your new world.
   > So; Easy, eh!   Si, Bon chance!

-Brian D'Arcy

The quantum Rapid!
More random than established tightly structured forms, and far more suited to our fragmented, sound-bitten times, Rapids jostle sets of often juxtaposed ideas. Densely packed semantics, tied together by a pincer movement of title and last line, explode upon observation to leave trails of understanding that belie their tiny size.

Consciousness in Waves

Semantic couplets   tiny nuggets
Bring purpose   once observed
Unread   their magic dies
Four lines foreshadow   comprehension
In gaps between   the real

Probably—No idea is of   itself, alone

-Jason Reading

What makes a good Rapid:

- First four lines should establish an atmosphere, intensely and variously, and the poem's concept, premise, statement, idea, or stage through disconnects or a single narrative. Try to create bounces.
- Fifth line will borrow the essence of the first four lines and develop it further to prepare for the sixth line. It is expected to create a separate tangent in a viewpoint established. Again to break a linear appearance of a poetic narrative.
- The sixth line can flow as a part of the fifth line or be an independent disconnect. You should add an extra tangent to the metaphor or an allegory, which should help enhance the meaning of all lines.
- In this sixth line, *the tabbed caesura occurs between the second and third stress*. This deliberate break creates two individual parts falling apart possibly with their own points!
- A title is a suggestive throwback of the poem's core idea, but mostly a twist as a metaphor or an idea: not a dull reaffirmation of the theme.
- The Rapid crystallizes an expression that would have been a longer poem.
- These poems are not linear, not like Tanka. They will fail as Rapids, if they have no disorientation language, metaphors, myths, etc.
- A fast pace is another reason what separates Rapids from other forms. Iambic pentameter is what our ears are trained to, while tetrameter and shorter trimeter are less in use. Sestets on their own are also considered as lower forms of poems by some academics! The form rebels against these traditionalist notions.

You will find some examples in the latest issue of the Pratik magazine.

-**YP**

Notes (2)
References

Actaeon: The hunter became the hunted; he was transformed into a stag, and Artemis's raging hounds, struck with a 'wolf's frenzy' (Lyssa), tore him apart as they would a stag." *(Courtesy of Wikipedia)*

ΔS ≥ 0: Delta S is always greater than or equal to zero: It is the equation of entropy. Like heat, time passes from disturbance to the order to upset the order. It is imagined that the emotional flow could be subject to the same rule of entropy.

404: An error page you land on when the link you clicked cannot find the webpage

Adikia: The Goddess of injustice in the Greek mythology, she is frequently depicted as a hideous woman with tattoos and throttles by Dike (see further up in the list).

Barbarians: Refers to the poem *Waiting for the Barbarians* by C. P. Cavafy

Bhavai is a traditional rich folk-theatre culture of Gujarat. (For **Ranglo**, see below)

Bhishma: A Hindu mythological figure from the epic Mahabharat, he was the son of the personification of the Ganges. He was the embodiment of oath fulfilled at all costs, even if it resulted in a disastrous outcome.

Chicken George: A character from Roots, an epic novel by Alex Haley. George was born out of repeated rapes of Kizzy, his mother. Promised his freedom from the slavery through his mastery of training roosters to fight for a win, he was ultimately cheated out of it.

Clotho: A Greek mythological figure, she spun the life of the mortals, including a decision on who would live or die.

Consequences is an old parlour game in a similar vein to the Surrealist game *exquisite corpse*. Each player is given a sheet of paper, and all are told to write a word or phrase to fit a description ("an animal"), optionally with some extra words to make the story. Each player then folds the paper over to hide the most recent line, and hands it to the next person. At the

end of the game, the stories are read out. *(Courtesy of Wikipedia)*
Crow: It refers to Crow (and its mythology) by Ted Hughes
Dike's staff: Dike is a Goddess of justice in the Greek mythology and depicted locked in dual with Adikia (see above), throttling and beating her with a staff. Carrying a balance scale in her hand, she is shown as a younger slim woman. She ruled over human justice.
Dragon's Gate: 1. In Greek mythology, Olympos (Olympus), the home of the gods was guarded with the golden gates with three Horai (Horae). 2. In Chinese mythology, the Dragon's Gate is located at the top of a waterfall cascading from a legendary mountain. If a carp successfully makes the jump, it is transformed into a powerful **dragon**.
Draupadi: In the game of dice, after losing himself as a stake, Yudhistir puts his wife Draupadi as a stake at the behest of a challenge by Duryodhana, and loses her too.
Duryodhana, overcome by humiliating Pandav, resorts to many insulting actions; the last one to make Draupadi naked in front of the onlookers in the court. Not protected by anyone, Krishna protects Draupadi with a constant spin of a sari to cover up her and exhaust Duryodhana's brother in the act. There are many complex arguments going on in the narrative created by the author of Mahabharata about morals, Dharma, etc. But for the reference here, this is the sari that appears in poems with its connotations.
Dvaita: A Vedic philosophy about the duality of soul (Atma) and the supreme soul (God, Parmatma). Gathering all experiences of reality, the soul that separated finally aims to merge back into the supreme soul. The philosophy explores separation and union. The One that is two and yet One.
Eeyore: A donkey from Winnie the Pooh, Eeyore, is generally portrayed as pessimistic and depressed.
Ego death is a "complete loss of subjective self-identity". In Jungian psychology, it is 'psychic death'.
Exquisite Corpse is a game in which a collection of words or images are collectively assembled. Each player adds to a composition in sequence, either by following a rule (e.g.
"The *adjective noun adverb verb* the *adjective noun*." as in "The green duck sweetly sang the dreadful dirge.") or by being allowed to

see only the end of what the previous person contributed. *(Courtesy of Wikipedia)*

The Galatea Effect is one of self-efficacy: the belief and trust in oneself and one's abilities and potential to succeed. Behind is a Greek myth, Pygmalion fell in love with an ivory statue he carved of a woman, so prayed to Aphrodite, who brought her to life. It represnts the effect as something that is not possible becomes possible.

Harmondsworth: A detention prison for the immigrants, but was also notorious for locking up the legal British Citizens of colour from the colony returning to Britain creating a dark and unwritten history of racism by the UK.

Jenga is a game of physical skill created by British board game designer and author Leslie Scott, and currently marketed by Hasbro. Players take turns removing one block at a time from a tower constructed of 54 blocks. Each block removed is then placed on top of the tower, creating a progressively more unstable structure. *(Courtesy of Wikipedia)*

Joseph K.: A character from Kafka's novel The Trial in which Joseph K. is arrested and prosecuted, not even he is ever told about his crime. Joseph K. becomes an object in an inhuman system with no other identity than the one accused.

Kalinga: The war King Ashoka fought only to be awakened to a higher cause or truth and Buddhism by realising war's brutality.

Khodumodumo: In African myth, it is a shapeless, voracious monster that swallows everything living it comes across.

Kisii: A town in Kenya

Kurukshetra: A battlefield featured in the epic Mahabharata

Kutzadika'a: A tribe living around the Mono Lake that eats its Flies

Lethe was one of the five rivers of the underworld of <u>Hades</u>. Also known as the *Ameles potamos* (river of unmindfulness), the Lethe flowed around the cave of <u>Hypnos</u> and through the Underworld where all those who drank from it experienced complete forgetfulness. Lethe was also the name of the Greek spirit of forgetfulness and oblivion, with whom the river was

often identified. *(Courtesy of Wikipedia)*
Lions of Sanchi Capital The Lion Capital of Ashoka is a sculpture of four Asiatic lions standing back to back symbolize preaching of 'the Four Noble Truths' of Buddhism and Dharma. A monument built by King Ashoka after the war of Kalinga. It has four lions for the four directions.

Meghadūta (Sanskrit: मेघदूत literally *Cloud Messenger*) is a lyric poem written by Kālidāsa (c. 4th–5th century CE), considered to be one of the greatest Sanskrit poets. It describes how a *yakṣa* (or nature spirit), who had been banished by his master to a remote region for a year, asked a cloud to take a message of love to his wife. The poem become well-known in Sanskrit literature and inspired other poets to write similar poems (known as "messenger-poems", or Sandesha Kavya) on similar themes. *(Courtesy of Wikipedia)*

Narad was god-sage who moved between heaven and earth, often bringing news from earth to Gods.

Orphic Egg: 1. The Orphic Egg in the Ancient Greek Orphic tradition is the cosmic egg from which hatched the primordial hermaphroditic deity Phanes/Protogonus (variously equated also with Zeus, Pan, Metis, Eros, Erikepaios and Bromius) who in turn created the other gods. The egg is often depicted with a serpent wound about it. *(Courtesy of Wikipedia)*   2. In Hindu mythology, the universe is called Brahmand meaning Lord Brahma's egg.

Psyche (Soul) was the most beautiful goddess. Eros fell in love with her instead of making her fall in love with some most hideous man he can find. Psyche was never allowed to see him. On advice of wicked sisters, she did. The betrayal came with a heavy price.

Psychopomps are creatures, spirits, angels, or deities in many religions whose responsibility is to escort newly deceased souls from Earth to the afterlife. Their role is not to judge the deceased, but simply to guide them. *(Courtesy of Wikipedia)*

Ranglo: In most Bhavai (see above) performances, Ranglo is a forestage character who, in between the acts, to change the monotony, entertains the audience with a laugh.

Radha is a Hindu Goddess and a consort of Lord Krishna. Her relationship to Krishna is interpreted in many ways. The Bollywood song with its first line referred here from Raj Kapoor's Satyam Shivam Sundaram is playful about Krishna's darker complexion. It celebrates the idea that love is not about colour prejudice.

Rudra Tandava: Shiva's destructive dance to bring in new creation.

Ruru: In Hindu mythology there is a love story of **Ruru** and his wife **Priyamvada**. Unfortunately, Priyamvada dies of snakebite. Ruru is lost without his wife. On invoking Yama, god of death, he begs for Priyamvada's life. Yama wants something in exchange. He offers half of his remaining life to his wife. And so it is done. Priyamvada returns to the living to live happily ever after.

Sestina: Altaforte Ezra Pound reading this poem as at https://www.openculture.com/2012/10/ezra_pounds_fiery_1939_reading_of_his_early_poem_isestina_altafortei.html captures the sound of him pounding on the table.

Shesh: Lord Vishnu is often depicted as resting on Shesha.

Spacetime cones: The temporal structure of the universe is made of cone shapes. Every event has its past, future and present represented as a cone. Light travels along the oblique lines to delimit these cones. They are also called 'light cones'. Without going into deep complex discussions, the mass of the black hole slows time at its border to stand still. The surface of the black hole aligns parallel to the edge of cones. This point where time stands still is also called 'the event horizon'. *(From The Order of Time by Prof Carlo Rovelli)*

SS Karanja: A passenger ship in the fifties from Kenya to India

Statue of Harmony: The statue of Sri Chinmoy posing with namaste in Prague along the river *Vltava*.

Surdarshana Chakra is a spinning-disc weapon of Vishnu and Krishna, His avatar.

The Bell Jar ID refers to Sylvia Plath's novel The Bell Jar and the identity crisis explored by the novel

The Book of Us by Andrea Michael

It is a story of friendship, love, betrayal, the healing power of forgiveness and much more.

The Galatea effect is an effect where one's own expectations or beliefs in their ability influence the positive outcome.

The Mono Lake flies: Read about the Mono Lake's bizarre alkali flies and its ecosystem at https://www.nationalgeographic.com/news/2017/11/diving-flies-mono-lake-underwater-spd/

The Myth of Sisyphus: Camu's philosophical essay on Absurdism compares the absurdity of Sisyphus's life from the Greek mythology to argue the point. Sisyphus condemned to repeat forever the same meaningless task of pushing a boulder up a mountain, only to see it roll down again.

Throbbers: The ring you see while you wait for a webpage to load.

Tsurara-onna: (つらら女, "icicle woman") is a Japanese folklore. It is a tale about an icicle that became a woman. A single man was looking at the icicles hanging under the eaves of his home and sighed saying "I'd like a wife as beautiful as these icicles," and just as he wished, a beautiful woman appeared who wanted to be his wife. This woman was an incarnation of an icicle, and there are variations on how this plays out. *(Courtesy of Wikipedia)*

Uncertainty principle: The quantum mechanics informs us about the fuzziness with which what we can know with certainty about the behaviour of quantum particles, and as a result about the smallest scale of nature. One cannot predict the value of a quantity with subjective certainty, even if all initial conditions are specific.

Vaitarani: A river in hell in Hinduism.

Yudhisthira अश्वत्थामा हतः इति नरो वा कुंजरो वाः Yudhistir is character from the epic Mahabharat and supposed to always tell the truth and represent what is right (Dharma). So, to cheat in the battlefield to make Drona lose Krishna's request him to shout a lie that Drona's son Ashwatthama has fallen. The line in Sanskrit is what he says in a quieter voice to himself: It can be a man or an elephant named Ashwatthama.

Zen(ī) is a crypto currency. In a game, Dragon Ball FighterZ, with the currency **Zeni** you can purchase anything from a new Fighter to Avatars; therefore gaining money in the game is a fairly important task. **Zen** with its root in Chinese chán and in Sanskrit (pronounced same) चेन्, also represents meditation, self-control or an understanding of our mind.

THE LONDON MAGAZINE

The London Magazine is England's oldest literary periodical, with a history stretching back to 1732. Today – reinvigorated for a new century – the Magazine's essence remains unchanged: it is a home for the best writing and an indispensable feature on the British literary landscape. Across a long life – spanning several incarnations – the pages of the Magazine have played host to a wide range of canonical writers, **from Percy Bysshe Shelley, William Hazlitt** and **John Keats** in the nineteenth century, to **T.S. Eliot, W.H. Auden** and **Evelyn Waugh** in the early twentieth century and, in recent decades the Magazine has published work by giants of contemporary fiction and poetry such as **William Boyd, Nadine Gordimer,** and **Derek Walcott.**

In February 1903, **H. G. Wells** published his first short story for the Magazine, Mr Skelmersdale in Fairyland. The London Magazine also published original stories from the likes of **Arthur Conan Doyle, Joseph Conrad, Jack London,** and **P. G. Wodehouse.** Thomas. T. S. Eliot recommended to readers "a magazine that will boldly assume the existence of a public interested in serious literature". **Louis MacNeice** published his Canto In Memoriam **Dylan Thomas,** and **Henry Green** reviewed the diaries of Virginia Woolf. The work of a vast array of towering twentieth-century figures found a home among its pages, including **William Burroughs, Harold Pinter, Ted Hughes, Sylvia Plath, Les Murray,** and **Paul Muldoon.**

Now, The London Magazine thrives under the editorship of **Steven O'Brien.**

Published six times a year, the Magazine is unmissable reading for anyone with an interest in literature, culture and ideas. Join a conversation that has endured for 300 years: subscribe today.

https://www.thelondonmagazine.org/subscription/